MODERN WISDOM

Wit, Wisdom and Thought-Provoking Ideas
for 21st Century Living

Copyright © 2025 Gene S. Jones

All rights reserved. No part of this publication may be reproduced, distributed, or transmitted in any form or by any means, including photocopying, recording, scanning or any other electronic or mechanical method, or by any information and retrieval system, without prior written permission from publisher.

Publisher's Cataloguing-in-Publication Data

Names:	Jones, Gene S., author.
Title:	Modern wisdom : wit, wisdom and thought-provoking ideas for 21st century living / Gene S. Jones.
Description:	First edition.	Katonah, New York : Dreamquest Publishing, [2025]	Includes bibliographical references.
Identifiers:	ISBN: 9780998324074	LCCN: 2025903886
Subjects:	LCSH: Self-help techniques—Quotations.	Life skills—Quotations.	Creative ability— Quotations.	Wisdom—Quotations.	Self-realization—Quotations.	Business—Quotations.	Spirituality—Quotations.	Success—Quotations.	Inspiration—Quotations.	Wit and humor—Quotations.	Philosophy—Quotations.	Human behavior—Quotations.	Interpersonal relations—Quotations.	Arts—Quotations.	LCGFT: Quotations.	BISAC: SELF-HELP / Affirmations.	PHILOSOPHY / Social	SELF-HELP / Personal Growth / General.
Classification:	LCC: PN6081 .J662 2025	DDC: 808.88/2--dc23

Front Cover Design: Barbara Aronica
Cover art: 3d kot/Shutterstock
Book Design: Carla Green
Editing: Kent Sorsky

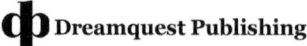

A Division of Royal Production Services, Inc.
P.O. Box 623
Katonah, New York 10536
www.dreamquestpublishing.com

Published in the United States of America

MODERN WISDOM

Wit, Wisdom and Thought-Provoking Ideas
for 21st Century Living

GENE S. JONES
Author of *Consolidated Wisdom*

Dreamquest Publishing

*Success is a goal.
Happiness is a state of mind.
Wisdom is the way.*

INTRODUCTION

This book has been assembled for one specific reason: To inspire you to think deeply, discuss ideas with others, and live a more fulfilling life. Although it seems impossible to get any meaningful agreement on the issues of our era, no matter what their beliefs, everyone I've spoken with over the past few years agrees that our world needs more wisdom. That universal sentiment has provided the impetus to organize my thoughts and offer *Modern Wisdom* to the world. Hopefully this book can help the world fill its need for greater understanding, compassion and wisdom.

    The writing down of my ideas began during freshman year in college, and that process has continued ever since. By serving in a variety of roles in the arts community, the sports community and the business community, I've learned what it feels like to be a performing artist, a director, a producer, a sports broadcaster, a CEO, and an arts administrator. My long career in the world of entertainment has introduced me to hundreds of thousands of fascinating people from all across the continental United States and the world, thereby exposing me to numerous cultures, wisdom traditions and ways of thinking. These interactions opened my eyes to the huge diversity of human experiences taking place simultaneously at every moment in every location on our planet.

The insights and advice offered in *Modern Wisdom* have all been inspired by conversations and situations I've found myself in, and relationships I've either witnessed first-hand or participated in... as opposed to stories I've been told by others. The phrases in the book are from conversations I've had with myself or words I've blurted out to others who immediately urged me to write them down lest I forget them. This is why I've always carried a notepad, although a smartphone recently replaced those notepads.

In reflection, I realize I'm a lifelong student of human nature who has given my mind the freedom to roam, explore and dig deeper... always fully surrendering to every project I work on. Continual full immersion is what helps me gain the greatest potential benefit from each experience. My journey began with a desire to make people smile, before evolving into a desire to make audiences laugh and then make them think. Now the desire is to enrich the lives of others. It is my heartfelt desire that the words of *Modern Wisdom* will enrich your life.

*My family is large,
because ideas are my children.*

Great ideas require love and nurture. In return,
they provide a special kind of companionship.

It's not necessary to touch someone's skin to get under it.

*Being in a hurry
doesn't get you there any faster.*

Those who are always in a hurry to get somewhere
are usually running away from something else.

*The middle of nowhere for everybody
is still somewhere special for somebody.*

The future always begins just now.

Every day is another opportunity to shape your destiny.

Something given and then taken away is more upsetting than something never owned.

You cannot miss what you never had.
Attachment creates vulnerability by
opening the door to the pain of detachment.

Home is wherever I sleep next to the one I love.

No matter where you are when you cut open a melon, fruit flies will appear.

Those who are most in need of advice are usually least willing to accept it.

*Logic was invented to explain
why human nature can be so illogical.*

If you always have to give in to fit in, then it's time to get out.

Compromise on issues and change with the times, but do not compromise your values, and do not overstay in a toxic situation.

Too much of a good thing can become a very bad thing.

One example is recent extended periods of gorgeous sunny days that led to serious drought and forest fires.

*A couple of great people
do not always make a great couple.*

Nothing speaks louder than a good listen. When we learn to listen, the whole world becomes our teacher.

The most important skill needed to become an effective talker or negotiator is learning to listen. People respond better once they feel heard and understood.

*The path to fulfillment
is rarely a straight line.*

Setbacks and failures are all part of the road
to success and fulfillment.

Never be different just to be different.

Be different to make a difference.

*The longer the silence,
the harder it is to break.*

*The only way to fully quiet the mind
is to fully express it.*

*The greatest accomplishment in life
is finding someone you love
who loves you the way you have always
dreamed of being loved.*

Lover's Proclamation:
You are the most unique and wonderful being I've ever met,
and I treasure every moment we spend together.

*If nobody can break your heart,
it's because they cannot find it.*

Make a commitment to your passions and remain passionate about your commitments.

The antidote for mid-life crisis is a mid-life renaissance.

PIE THEORY

Whenever there is a "pie" to be divided, the concept should be one of working together to make the pie larger rather than worrying about how to divide it up.

*It doesn't matter what you choose to do.
What matters is how much love
you do it with.*

Every effort is improved by the presence of love.

Self-praise arises from self-doubt.

If you doubt yourself, everyone else will too.

*The bridge to the future
can also be a tunnel to the past.*

Don't allow anxiety about the future drag you back to your past. Rather, decipher wisdom from the past and apply it to future endeavors. Fully in the moment is the only place to be.

Today fully lived leads me boldly into the future. Today not fully lived slides me back to the past.

Each present moment contains every previous moment, and present moments build the future. When regrets from the past are allowed to collide with anxiety about the future, the present disappears. The only certain reality is the present moment. All else is either memory or speculation.

*It's amazing what you can find
when you're looking for something else.*

Many great inventions and innovations have been developed accidentally while their creators were striving for a different result. This exemplifies the importance of sustained effort, as persistent searches often unearth surprising gems.

No thought is unheard and no prayer goes unanswered, although not always in the way we expect or recognize.

This is the essence of faith.
Faith also needs an action plan.

Affluence legitimizes eccentricity.

Parents who give their children everything they ask for will raise unhappy children.

. . . because those who are given everything they want will always want more than they ever have.

*Great loss is an invitation
to divine inspiration.
Every pain has a story to tell.
That is the gift of pain.*

The great challenge of physical and emotional pain is the journey to find their gifts or let their gifts find you. Self-pity blocks this transformative process. The profound lesson of gratitude is learning to become genuinely grateful for all your difficulties and problems, which is why *gratitude is the best attitude*.

"I'm not afraid of what you think of me"
doesn't mean
"I don't care what you think of me."

Lack of fear does not necessarily imply ambivalence.

The healer is healed while healing others.

When practiced at its highest level, the art of healing
also has a healing effect on the healer.

*Dreading disaster
is often worse than experiencing it.*

Paranoia can become a self-fulfilling prophecy.

Fear becomes the largest roadblock on the path to success when it stifles attempts to achieve greatness.

Only argue with people you respect.

Acts of kindness that only take a few seconds of your time can resonate in their recipients for a lifetime.

Every display of kindness has greater value than can be initially observed.

*An attempt to be all things to all people
is the quickest route to
the superhighway of mediocrity.*

Be true to yourself, rather than worrying
about the opinions of others.

If you hold your clients to the same high standards they hold you to, most will leave you.

A true sign of compassion is when someone hurts you, rather than attempt to hurt them in return, you attempt to understand their situation.

Keep asking questions, because your first good idea is rarely the best one.

There is a question embedded in every answer, and an answer residing in every question. It's best to answer all questions, and then question all your answers.

*These days, it takes so much more
to have it all.*

Happiness is not having all you want
. . . it's appreciating what you have.
Awareness is knowing the difference
between what you want and what you need.

Happiness is doing a favor for someone when it's really what you want to do in the first place.

Anyone who thinks they have it all is missing a lot. Someone who thinks they know it all is definitely misinformed.

When everyone around you always seems wrong . . . it's actually you.

When the whole world seems wrong from your position,
it's time to change your position and take a long look
in the proverbial mirror. Bear in mind that
If everyone is driving you crazy, you are probably already there.

*Exceptions once granted
expand endlessly.*

Heroes in search of recognition often create victims to rescue.

When you are angry with someone else, you are usually in some way also angry at yourself.

*Smiles that say maybe
also say maybe not.*

The word "maybe" is the apparel of the ambivalent.

Loneliness never gets tired.

It's essential to acknowledge your weaknesses in order to overcome them.

Acknowledging your weaknesses is a sign of strength.

*An average is only a statistic
. . . not a reality.*

If you cannot be happy unless you succeed, then you probably still won't be happy after you succeed.

Rapid success is also a time for caution.

Success is determined by how much we learn from our failures. Those who succeed often have had more failures than those who fail.

There are hidden gifts in all failures and setbacks. They illuminate the need for change while teaching us lessons we need to learn. Tragedy comes not from suffering setbacks but from failure to learn their lessons. Understanding the "why" of failures is a key to eventual success. When approached with perseverance and flexibility, the details of a failure can create possibilities for better outcomes.

The first step to getting somewhere is the decision you're not willing to stay where you are.

Dissatisfaction with the status quo
is a prime motivator of change.

When one door closes, another door opens, but those who look too long at the closed door fail to see the one that just opened for them.

Continually be on the lookout for new opportunities.
It's not their job to look for you.

*Work from the heart,
and your wallet will swell.*

This is the benefit of doing work that you love.

He who has struggled is best able to help he who is struggling.

Struggle generates understanding and compassion for others.

*Learning to shut out the noise
inadvertently shuts out some of the music.*

*Beware the self-destructive aspects
of the pursuit of leisure.*

Rock bottom presents a great opportunity to rise up.

All setbacks have silver linings.

It's our responsibility to find them and take action.

Sympathy without respect is an insult.

Even in defeat, goodness is a winner.

More insidious than the infliction of guilt is the infliction of doubt.

*Too late is when yesterday was
the last time everything was possible.*

It's a pity that full understanding
so often arrives a day after too late.

The selfish can never be satisfied.

*When others mistreat you,
never let them know that you know,
or else they will never forgive you.*

When egos prevail, friendships do not.

*Those who avoid responsibility
never receive its rewards.*

*If you make a promise, write it down
as a reminder to keep every promise
you make . . . to always
do what you say you will do.*

Forgotten promises erode trust.
Being dependable puts you on the path to success.
This is the Art of the Follow-Through.

Adventurous discovers,
Genius invents,
Creativity improves,
Greatness unites.

Command of more than one of these four
attributes is a major accomplishment.

Luck is a skill enhanced by the power of observation.

The key to improving your luck is learning to recognize the opportunities life presents before they disappear.

Flamboyance is rarely what it looks like.

Flamboyance often disguises great inner turmoil.

*The guilty are always suspicious
and the suspicious are often guilty.*

Generosity is its own reward.

Giving from the heart can bestow great pleasure
on all participants.

*The person who has least
is one who finds nothing inside to give.*

We all have something to give, even if that gift is not tangible. Love is the greatest gift, and all of us possess the ability to give love, whether or not we choose to do so.

Those who make no mistakes usually make few discoveries.

Fear of making mistakes is a roadblock to progress.

Those who do not learn from their mistakes cannot afford to make any.

Your problems can become your greatest assets.

Never overlook the opportunities hidden inside a problem.

The greatest cause of large problems is small ones. Ignore them at your own risk.

*Complainers never fix.
Fixers do not complain.*

Would you rather complain . . .
or solve your problems?

Information overloads can block the path to the solution of a problem.

Clarity is best achieved from simplicity.
Clutter tends to cloud the landscape.
Be selective in choosing input materials.

The problem is always part of the solution and the solution is always part of a new problem. Don't live in the problem . . . live in the solution.

Focus on where you are going, not where you've been.
Dig deeper by asking more questions.

Complex problems need not require complicated solutions. When possible, simplify problems with focus and perseverance.

This can be called *The Law of Paradoxical Simplification*.

A debt promptly repaid becomes an asset.

. . . because it establishes trust.

*In times of rapid change,
the status quo is a guaranteed loser.*

... but every change needs a valid reason.

Perfectionism is often procrastination in disguise.

Have you ever postponed starting something
until everything is just right?
Don't allow your preparation to stretch into procrastination.

The Art of Positive Procrastination is doing something positive while procrastinating about doing something else.

Much can be accomplished while your mind is in this modality.

Those who strive for perfection always fail to achieve it, as perfection is not a sustainable condition, although greatness is often a by-product of the effort.

All perfect moments are fleeting. Also, perfection is a judgment made by imperfect people, so it's therefore imperfect. Although it's an unobtainable goal, perfection is a wonderfully motivating target to aspire to.

The most precarious human condition is contentment.

Never become complacent when things are going well.
It requires the same effort and vigilance to maintain success as
to achieve it. The same is true for interpersonal relationships.

If you feel the need to ask a lot of questions about your love relationship, then the answers will probably not be what you want to hear.

If you realize someone is loving you for the wrong reason, look in the mirror, because it's likely you are also loving them for the wrong reason.

A weak species must become inventive to survive. Therefore, weaker species become more creative or perish.

Prehistoric humans developed creativity to compensate for their fragility while fighting for survival in the animal kingdom. Sharks have never needed to be creative since they are superior predators. This can be called
The Law of Evolutionary Dysfunction.

A fantasy shared becomes reality.

Never underestimate the companionship of a dream.
Pursue your dreams, but never confuse living with dreaming.
One who dreams of tomorrow must also live for today.

FIREFLY RULE OF CREATIVITY

Capturing genius or creativity out of thin air is much like catching fireflies in an empty mayonnaise jar at night. If you capture one tiny firefly, there will be one tiny beam of light in your jar. Each additional firefly adds one more tiny beam of light. If you catch enough fireflies, your jar will be brightly illuminated. Someone who does not bother to pursue those tiny fireflies and instead waits to catch one huge firefly, sits all night with a dark jar.

It's often an accumulation of numerous small thoughts and ideas that lead to big breakthroughs. Embracing all ideas to build significant change is "living the process."

Art is the conversion of fantasies and dreams into reality through forms that others can observe as reality and then convert into their own fantasies and dreams.

Great performances and art are initially personal, but evolve to become universal.

*Creativity can be learned.
Creativity can be taught.*

There are two fundamental types of creativity: Artistic Creativity and Practical Creativity. Although not everyone is artistic, everyone can learn to be more creative in dealing with the challenges of everyday life and solving problems.

The art of poetry is an ability to make a point without ever stating what it is.

Great art depicts the suffering of its era.

Creativity is what enables humans to transform suffering into art.

A true artist always remains a student of his craft.

The same is true for teachers in all disciplines.

Live your life as if it were a work of art.

*The key to your success
will be your response to pressure.*

An ability to perform under pressure is
the truest sign of mastery.

Mastery is a spiritual experience.

Mastery provides the skill to consistently achieve one's desired result regardless of circumstance. The greatest reward of mastery is the beauty and pleasure it provides to others.

Mastery arises from the repetition of excellence. Therefore, repetition is the key to mastery.

This implies that the key to mastery is relentless practice, a corollary to the well-known phrase practice makes perfect. The process of achieving mastery teaches lessons far beyond the skill being mastered, as the path to mastery is a process that becomes applicable to all other future endeavors.

Always exceed your talents with your goodness. Make sure your heart is always bigger than your ego. Beware of the blind spots of virtuosity.

Virtuosity with heart is far greater than simple virtuosity. Never lose touch with your heart while gaining skill and recognition. Do not allow virtuosity to cloud your understanding of how difficult it is to achieve. Humbleness and compassion are always important complementary assets.

Spontaneity is a profound discipline.

It takes much preparation, training, and experience
to be productively spontaneous in any arena of life.

If you are spending time attempting to think out of the box, then you have already boxed yourself in.

It is best to leave all your boxes behind
when seeking creative solutions.

*Periodically soaring above the clouds
or swept under the rug,
a creative life knows no middle road.*

Although one's creative self tends to be one's best self,
living a creative life can be a roller coaster ride at times.

Great ideas need to be followed by effective action.

Rules are meant to be bent . . . not broken.

Good and effective rules possess flexibility
so they can adapt to changing times and conditions.

*Why is it I feel most intelligent
when asking questions . . .
not when offering answers?*

*The seminal tool of learning
is the question.*

Humans are inquisitive by nature. The quest to learn begins at birth. As soon as a baby learns to talk, it begins asking questions, not spouting answers.

How you learn is just as important as what you learn. Intermingling education with entertainment and the art of play enhances the learning process.

Learning is a process, not an entity. The ultimate goal of learning reaches far beyond the accumulation of information . . . it is understanding and wisdom. Education is at its best when students are taught how to think and become inspired to grow both intellectually and socially.

While teaching a lesson, a great teacher simultaneously learns a different lesson.

A teacher's depth and understanding of a subject grows during the act of transmitting knowledge. Great teachers go beyond lesson plans to teach students how to learn.

Always be willing to live the life you teach.

Nostalgia is life's replacement for passion.

*The price of fame
is unlimited vulnerability.*

The cost of invulnerability is isolation.

However, isolation is much more tolerable when self-imposed.

Never seek approval from those who tend to withhold it.

. . . because you will forfeit your personal power.

Never give advice in order to impress yourself.

We all walk aimlessly down the directionless path as if there was a map.

Every life blazes its own unique path.
There is no road map to find the route to your destiny.

The burden of wealth is that you have more to lose.

Prosperity can also be a source of anxiety.

*Great warriors never fight **against** anything . . . they always fight **for** what they believe in.*

This may seem like a purely semantic argument, as fighting for justice is also a fight against injustice, but there is a significant difference. Fighting for something establishes a goal. Fighting for something allows warriors to know when goals have been achieved, so they can either rest or move on.

*An enemy of my enemy
may also be my enemy.*

This is an unfortunate reality in both geopolitics and personal relationships. It eclipses the adage an enemy of my enemy is my friend, which has often been proven to be incorrect, as alliances built on shared enmity are always precarious and unstable. If you embrace the concept of an enemy of your enemy being your friend, you may end up with 'friends' who are simply enemies who hate a common enemy more than they hate you.

Never fight an enemy who has nothing to lose.

The greatest weapon against an enemy who has nothing to lose is a gift they will treasure greatly . . . hence, something they don't want to lose.

Although they usually end with peace treaties, wars never end in the hearts and minds of their combatants and descendants.

Resentments are not erased by peace treaties. A study of history reveals that many wars of the distant past are still being fought, as they linger in the minds of both the vanquished and the victors. Like fireplace embers waiting for a future spark to combust, ancestral grudges churn endlessly.

While there are no politics in wisdom, hopefully someday there will be more wisdom in politics.

It's quite apparent most politicians become significantly wiser immediately after retiring from politics, as the political process distorts their logic while they are immersed in it.

The first step toward winning the Nobel Peace Prize is starting a war you know how to end.

Determination is the fuel of perseverance.

These are two powerful ingredients of long-term success.

*Rest is a key component
of sustainable productivity.*

Diverse groups are most easily unified by a universal symbol. The more universal the symbol, the wider its appeal. Unfortunately, seeking wider appeal dilutes the purity of symbols, eventually causing followers of such symbols to quarrel and splinter.

To be effective, societal symbols need to have widely accepted meanings attached to them.

*Those who suffer gracefully
shall be rewarded greatly.*

Grace will be rewarded.
The essential word here is patience.
Patience makes time your friend.

*The quickest way to lose friends
is by pointing out their imperfections.*

Always be older than you look and younger than you act.

Maturity is ageless.

May the young become wiser and may the elders retain their youthfulness as these two cycles of life intersect to create greater awareness, compassion, prosperity and happiness for the world.

Time and experience round the edges of our personalities like wind and water smooth a stone.

We cannot build a perfect future for our youth, but we can help perfect our youth for their future.

*Always live in the "is"
... not in the "should."*

Should is not a word that respects reality.
What should be . . . already is.

Anything that is timely soon becomes obsolete.

This highlights the distinction between being timely versus being timeless.

*Every era has its dinosaur
blindly heading toward extinction.*

Will humans join this category?
Has the process already begun?

*To change your way,
it's essential to change your ways.*

Internal change is often necessary to manifest tangible change.
Positive change requires adaptive behavior.

To get what you want, you must be clear about expressing what you want.

This highlights the importance of clarity, as defining a goal is the first step toward achieving it. It's then necessary to make our desires known if we want them to find support. In turn, our odds of encountering good luck along the way will be greatly improved.

If you can imagine it, you can do it.

The impossible becomes possible once you figure out
how to divide it into achievable components.
Nothing is impossible for those who never stop trying.

*Luck is a talent, so put in the work
to create your own good luck.*

When perceived in this manner, luck becomes a learnable skill
linked to our powers of observation. The question is:
How many opportunities have you missed in your lifetime?

When a prisoner gains the respect of his captor, the captor becomes the prisoner.

This is a warning to all captors,
and a ray of hope for all prisoners.

Worry is a burden on the person being worried about.

This is why worriers should keep their worry to themselves.

*Inaction is a choice.
Just like any action,
inaction has its risks and rewards.*

Wisdom assists us to accurately evaluate
the balance between action and inaction.

*Am I truly alive,
or am I my own imagination
. . . or can both be true?*

In the narrowest sense, all we see are projections of our own desire. If we are hungry, we only see signs for restaurants. If our car is running out of gas, we only see gas station signs. As encapsulated by Abraham Maslow, if you're a hammer, everything you see looks like a nail.

*Nature is much greater than what transpires on planet Earth.
Nature is the whole Universe.
Nature is intergalactic.*

Did you wake up more tired than when you went to bed?

Maybe you were abducted!

Make sure what you are living for doesn't kill you.

Remember that the career you choose will eventually shape who you become. Authentic success needs to include a balanced life.

Careers can have multiple agendas, but those agendas must blossom from the core of one sustaining concept like leaves and branches supported by the trunk of a nurturing tree.

In all aspects of life, find your source and find your center . . . especially in your career.

Optimism is a self-fulfilling prophecy.

... because optimism breeds perseverance,
and expectations create reality.

Before accusing someone of being hot under the collar, make sure you're not breathing down their neck.

Choose the words you say to yourself with great care.

The power of words applies not only to what we say to others but also to ourselves, so replace all negatives with words of positivity.

When someone says,
"I'm doing the best I can"
... you both know it's not true.
When someone says,
"It's not about the money"
... it always is.
When someone says,
"I don't want to hurt you"
... they already have, and they will hurt you again.
When someone says,
"Nothing can ever change the way I feel about you"
... something already has.

These are living examples of the classic phrase
"actions speak louder than words."

*The foolish are constantly surprised
by the obvious.*

Throw out something old every year.

Getting rid of the old makes room for something new to enter. Possession of clear space is a valuable asset.

THE TRUTH ABOUT TRUTH

*Truth transcends process.
Being right for the wrong reason is still right.
Being wrong for the right reason is still wrong.
Never allow process to cloud the truth.
The search for the truth is
as precious as its possession.
When the truth is unpopular, so are those who tell it.
The most insidious dishonesty
is a carefully twisted truth.
All great truths are simple.
It's the distortions of truth that become complicated.*

*Hard Truths are tangible and measurable.
They can be verified.
Soft Truths are generally true,
but also possess elements of subjectivity.
Liquid Truths are largely or totally subjective
and vary due to competing opinions,
interpretations, and biases.*

Liquid and Soft Truths have always been debated, but the current upheaval in society has been fueled by an erosion of a fundamental agreement on the validity of Hard Truths, thereby causing Hard Truths to be conflated with Liquid and Soft Truths.

Facts can be a severe constraint upon the imagination.

*The secret of intimacy
is keeping no secrets.*

Keeping secrets destroys intimacy. Sharing secrets builds intimacy. The great surrender in a love relationship is the sharing of your inner sanctum.

Courage depends on fear for its existence.

If no fear needs to be overcome, then courage has no basis for existence, as courage can only be measured by the amount of fear and danger it encounters.

Greatness is relative.

Greatness needs comparison to be fully validated.

True greatness never needs to brag.

Bragging is a symptom of inner disharmony.

*Justice is never served
by the assignment of blame.*

Never use blame as a weapon,
and never blame others for your shortcomings.

*Never allow others
to distort your self-image.*

Strong intuition deserves strong consideration.

Never let intuition be blocked by circumstance. Don't allow stress to cloud your judgment or paralyze your thinking.

*An extraordinarily loud laugh
is often a geyser of unhappiness.*

All great humor contains an element of truth and wisdom.

Nonsense makes sense when it can be enjoyed.

*If you have no expectations,
you cannot be disappointed.*

Expectations can also plant seeds of disappointment.

*Embrace constructive criticism
as an opportunity for growth.*

Forgiving others and admitting when you're wrong are signs of strength.

*The reason for living does not exist.
We must create reasons for ourselves.*

The paradox is that all perceived meaning is artificial
. . . but also important.

The quicker someone can sum up the meaning of life, the less it means to them.

Only the dead live forever.

Death is the beginning of immortality.

Television has no conscience.

This is only one small example of the absence of compassion in technology and why technology should be viewed as a tool, not a way of life.

OPPOSITES

Every reward has a hidden cost.
Every setback has a silver lining.
Every rise to power possesses
seeds of destruction.
Every fall is an opportunity to rise.
Every question has an answer.
Every answer contains a question.

Opposites provide important balance to existence.

*He who has no hope has no shame,
and he who has no shame is dangerous.*

This is why it's essential to provide hope
to all those who have lost it.

*The road to fulfillment
travels through the heart.*

Never offer to do that which you cannot do with a happy heart.

If you find a coin in the street, it's there for a reason. If it's face up, it's for you. Take it, make a wish, then give it away. If it's face down, it's for you to turn over and leave for someone else.

While we all are delighted to find money in the street that others have lost or misplaced, we rarely know when we may have lost some of our own money. Is it possible you have lost as much as you have found?

When you make a wish, mean it. Envision it as your lottery ticket.

Envisioning desires is the first step toward manifesting them.

*The only dreams that last forever
are those that never come true.*

Never shut down your dreams. Welcome them, study them,
and provide them opportunities to grow.

Any path worth taking will present obstacles you must overcome.

How much are you willing to sacrifice to
manifest your dreams and achieve your goals?
It requires commitment and hard work
to make dreams come true.

Endless difficulties brew indifference.

Indifference has the ability to inflict as much pain as hatred.

*The hardest, most impenetrable shell
is worn by someone who was
sensitive once and found it to no avail.*

Simple apologies can appear hollow. The sincerity of an apology is validated by action.

When someone makes a meaningful adjustment based on an apology, or when a company takes appropriate corrective action, the apology is validated. A mutually agreeable action based on an apology can create a lasting bond between the two participating parties. This is a way for companies to build customer loyalty and for interpersonal relationships to grow.

A teacher of hate is inevitably its recipient.

The person who won this year's Busiest Person of the Year Award was too busy to accept it.

Never be busy just to be busy. Being perpetually busy is often the manifestation of avoidance behavior . . . avoidance of doing something else that is actually more important but appears painful or overwhelming in some way. Being busy is the near enemy of accomplishment. It's not always a sign that progress is being made. Never mistake hyperactivity for accomplishment.

*Nonstop questioning tends to obscure the answer...
until the questioner stops talking.*

Let your questions breathe,
if you want to receive a proper answer.

*For a perpetual traveler,
the journey is home.
For the entertainer,
the stage is home.*

Where is your home?

The true art of loving is to love others the way they want to be loved.

There's so much more to the art of loving than love itself.
It's essential to learn your partner's "love language"
and treat that knowledge with respect and affection.
At the same time, it's essential to express your own love
language so your partner knows how to go about loving you.
Also, make sure you are in love with your partner and not
mistakenly infatuated with their amorous feelings for you.

*True love's most enduring gift
is unwavering devotion.*

Those who seek emotional safety in love are guaranteed to find disappointment.

Never allow fear to move you away from love.
Never choose safety over love.

*Those who always follow the advice
"better safe than sorry"
eventually become sorry they are so safe.*

Never choose safety over living fully.
Life is not designed to be a safe journey . . .
after all, it's guaranteed to end in death.

CIRCLE OF THE SELF

May the universe lead you to your true self,
May your true self lead you
to your true calling,
May your true calling lead you
to your true love,
May love teach you to love your true self.

Circles represent the interconnectedness of all things, and many journeys that come "full circle" lead you back to your true self. If you cannot understand who you've been, you'll never understand who you've become.

*We must learn to love
even that which we cannot control.*

Surrendering to love allows it to flow. Find a
way to love everyone and everything in your life,
even your opponents and enemies.

Chaos is an essential component of creativity. The linear mind finds comfort in order. The creative mind finds inspiration in chaos.

The innate desire to resolve chaos is a driver of creativity. Creative minds seek or create chaos for the opportunity to resolve it. Short-term chaos can be a catalyst for productive change, but lingering chaos is an invitation for long-term dysfunction.

FREEDOM, FORCE, AND CHAOS

Suffering through chaos in the pursuit of freedom is well worth the ordeal.

Only through the initial chaos created by the presence of freedom can sustainable order be achieved without force.

Restrictions have no merit until the limits of freedom have been explored.

Abuse of freedom is as ugly as a lack of it.

*Those who seize control by force
will inevitably be dethroned by force.
The greater the effort to control,
the greater the eventual chaos.*

The imposition of force often leads to unintended consequences. Those who seek to impose order by force unwittingly become the creators of extreme chaos inversely proportional to their effort to control.

The Bear Trap of History occurs when all efforts to control meet with the universe's drift toward greater entropy. History is replete with examples demonstrating that the greater the effort to control, the greater the eventual chaos before the chaos finally resolves into a new form of organization.

The repercussions of large-scale control often take time to manifest. This lag time often seduces despots and authoritarian leaders into shortsighted power grabs that lead to an inevitable demise of their regimes and empires. The more a nation seeks to control, the deeper its eventual ruin will be. It may take years, decades, or even centuries, but history assures us it will happen. Meanwhile, the collateral damage can be devastating.

Absolute power eventually self-destructs.

History teaches us that the quicker a despot's rise to power, the quicker the fall.

*The edge of destruction can also be
the verge of enlightenment.*

Control over oneself is the only true control one can possess. Control over others is either temporary or an illusion . . . or both.

*At every moment in time,
the process of evolution
proceeds invisibly.*

Evolution can only be evaluated by looking backward,
and the final stage of evolution is always extinction.

History is the greatest mystery.

Mankind still does not know
the totality of its prehistoric origin.

Every event and major decision made during any period in history has repercussions that may manifest hundreds or even thousands of years later. The goal for every society should be to decipher the lessons of history and move in a more sensible direction.

An extremely important aspect of history is its profound connection to the future. History actually determines the future by providing a foundation for present activities. This serves as a stern warning for those who believe we can ignore history, as doing so has always been a treacherous miscalculation.

Humanity always needs a new frontier.

A scarcity of frontiers leads to conflict,
causing humanity to turn on itself.

*Today's rebels
will become tomorrow's establishment.*

The greatest challenge of a revolution begins after it succeeds.

Crowding increases stress, hostility, and mindlessness.

This highlights everyone's need for a personal sanctuary.

If you want others to do something your way, convince them they thought of it first, and then be resigned to the fact you'll never get the credit.

Removing your ego from a negotiation facilitates superior solutions. This is the key to results-based thinking that leads to win-win situations. The lesson is to be satisfied in knowing you have succeeded in getting your idea accepted.

*One cannot fix oneself
by attempting to fix the world.*

Such an attempt merely brings on a temporary illusion
of well-being. Before venturing forth to fix the world, first
fix yourself... and if you become busy caring for the world,
be careful it doesn't run you over.

*Time does not actually exist,
but eternity does. Time is mankind's
artificial subdivision of eternity.*

Time is how humans divide up eternity.
Eternity divided by 5 = Eternity.
Eternity times 5 = Eternity.
The above equations demonstrate how time is an arbitrary
measurement of a nonexistent entity we all adhere to . . .
mankind's calibration of eternity we've been trained to accept.

The only necessary qualification for being a loser is believing you are one.

*Any fool with a match
can burn down the whole forest.*

It's so much easier to destroy than to build.

Purity is an essential element of beauty.

Purity is a quality that can be felt on a deeply emotional level.

Sit in stillness until you learn to enjoy it.

This is the basis for meditation.
The best peace is internal.

*Style must always yield to substance.
Flash needs to be supported by
fundamentals.*

Style without substance is hollow.
Style when supported by substance is sublime.

*When the clothes make the man,
they haven't got much to work with.*

Clothes are merely decorations. Interpretations of fashion statements are in the eyes of the beholders, and not always what the wearer intended.

Ignorance is the strongest opinion.

Ignorance is an essential ingredient of arrogance. Unfortunately, people tend to disagree with what they cannot understand.

Skillful speakers can make you love them, but great ones can help you love yourself.

*You can only love someone else
as much as you love yourself.*

*The only way to fully receive love
is to give yourself fully.*

Surrender is the key to receiving love. We must learn to love that which we cannot control in order to receive the full benefits of love.

*If you love your beloved every day
as if they may die tomorrow,
then your love will live forever.*

Every moment without love is a precious moment forever lost.

The most direct way to experience the soul of another is through their passion.

Sharing similar passions is a natural way
to build meaningful relationships.

*Being consistent
doesn't have to always be the same.
Remember:
The same doesn't look the same
after a while.*

Sometimes different approaches are needed to gain the same desired results. This highlights the value of mental flexibility.

The happiest endings never end

. . . they endure as fond memories.

MORNING PRAYER

*Thank you for this day.
I will make the most of it I possibly can.
May I have the wisdom, strength, and
fortitude to live this day with grace.*

EVENING PRAYER

*Thank you for this day.
May this night's sleep help me process
all I have learned during my waking hours.*

Gratitude is the best attitude.

. . . because gratitude clears the mind of negative thoughts.

AFFIRMATION BUFFET

My goal is to be a harmonious human.
In every moment, I am where I am supposed to be.
I accept the consequences of my actions.
Every setback is an opportunity to learn
and improve myself.
I will find reasons to be grateful every day.
Each loss creates space for a future success.
I am succeeding at being myself.
I will be fully present for every person
with whom I spend time.
I do not need more than I have.
I will unearth and develop my inner greatness,
and use that greatness for the benefit of others.
I will never use blame as a weapon.
When problems arise, I will focus on
finding solutions . . . not excuses.
I realize that what is, is meant to be.

MEETINGS WITH MYSELF

One sunny summer afternoon, while on a leisurely countryside stroll, I noticed a dead raccoon upside down on the side of a road, his bloated body reclined in a permanently rigid repose. The scene of this poor creature's demise filled me with a sudden epiphany that this raccoon was actually me from a previous lifetime, a notion leading to the stunning realization that perhaps I was one of the original amoebas on Earth four billion years ago and have been wandering through thousands of lifetimes on this planet after surviving many lifetimes on other worlds to arrive at this specific time and place . . . the revelation of my previously undisclosed ancient ancestry.
Upon returning home, I pondered this unsettling experience while sitting alone in my backyard, until a butterfly floated by. . . and once again I saw myself.

THE WORLD WE CANNOT SEE

The world we cannot see is all around us.
It's the world of dreams and hopes where all wishes come true
and love is always in the air.

The world we cannot see can see us more clearly
than we see ourselves.
It knows what's best for us, but cannot speak,
so the wisdom of the sky remains in the clouds,
constantly yearning to rain some advice our way.

The world we cannot see wonders
why we only look skyward when the sun is shining,
unaware that lightning, wind, blizzards, and rain
are messengers of the divine released for our benefit.

The world we cannot see is the real world,
the heart of the universe pulsing in every celestial object
and creature on our planet, so what we see
is merely a minuscule version of the expansive unknown.
Fortunately for us, what we see
suffices to provide us sustenance and the nagging intuition
that there's always something new to learn
from the world we cannot see.

When translated into action, wisdom phrases become valuable survival skills.

The power of a wisdom phrase is determined by
its ability to inspire productive positive action.
Creativity enhances the effectiveness of actionable wisdom

*Fads come and go,
mountains may crumble,
and even the sky may fall,
but wisdom will always be in style.*

This book is dedicated to the charismatic mentors who helped shape my journey through life, and all the fascinating people I've encountered during my five-decade career in the world of entertainment.

Special thanks to:

Bob Siroka for teaching me the practice of psychodrama and being my trusted advisor for more than forty years.

Peter Andrews for giving me my first job in the music business and putting me on stage for the first time.

Jango Edwards for showing me the roadmap to express myself as an entertainer.

Carlo Mazzone-Clementi, my commedia dell'arte mentor who taught me how to be an authentic stage performer.

Milt Larsen for inviting me to be part of his quest to preserve the variety arts and introducing me to some of history's greatest vaudeville entertainers.

Thomas Ashley-Farrand for being my spiritual teacher.

Gelmu Sherpa for initiating me into the practice and traditions of playing Tibetan bowls.

Jonathan Goldman for inspiring me to become a sound healing practitioner.

David Boehm for bringing me in to work at the *Guinness Book of World Records*.

Most of all to my father, who taught me the value of patience, perseverance and integrity.

BIBLIOGRAPHY

Anything that is timely soon becomes obsolete.
    From *Sunday's Mail*, by Gene S. Jones (1988)

The hardest, most impenetrable shell is worn by someone who was sensitive once and found it to no avail.
    From *Sunday's Mail*

Any fool with a match can burn down the whole forest.
    From *Sunday's Mail*

Soaring above the clouds or swept under the rug, a creative life knows no middle road.
    From *Younger and Wiser: Peaceful Words for a Troubled World*, by Gene S. Jones (2020)

The only dreams that last forever are those that never come true.
    From *Younger and Wiser*

May the young become wiser and may the elders retain their youthfulness as these two cycles of life intersect to create greater awareness, compassion, prosperity, and happiness to the world.
    From *Younger and Wiser*

An enemy of my enemy may also be my enemy.
    From *Younger and Wiser*

Those who seek emotional safety in love are guaranteed to find disappointment.
   From *Younger and Wiser*

These days, it takes so much more to have it all.
   From "Tree of More," in *Younger and Wiser*

To change your way, it is essential to change your ways.
   From "Are We the Goat?" in *Younger and Wiser*

Thank you for this day. I will make the most of it I possibly can. May I have the wisdom, strength, and fortitude to live this day with grace.
   From *Younger and Wiser*

Fads come and go, mountains may crumble, and even the sky may fall, but wisdom will always be in style.
   From *Consolidated Wisdom*, by Gene S. Jones (2024)

ABOUT THE AUTHOR

Gene S. Jones has lived a profoundly eclectic life. His five-decade career in the world of entertainment has included a wide range of exploits, including notable credits as a game show host, producer, director, speech writer, character actor, sportscaster, professional juggler, fire-eater, creativity coach, arts administrator, sound healer, and former Associate Editor of *The Guinness Book of World Records*.

Other books by Gene S. Jones:
Sunday's Mail

Younger and Wiser: Peaceful Words for a Troubled World

Consolidated Wisdom: The Ultimate Book of Quotations for Success, Happiness, and Health

For more information about Gene S. Jones, visit his websites:

genejoneswisdom.com

gimmeahint.com

www.ingramcontent.com/pod-product-compliance
Lightning Source LLC
Chambersburg PA
CBHW081155020426
42333CB00020B/2508